Walk for the Show

TIMOTHY WAYNE RYDER

Copyright

FriesenPress

Suite 300 – 852 Fort Street
Victoria, BC, Canada V8W 1H8

www.friesenpress.com

Distributed to the trade by The Ingram Book Company

Rick Rose;

Happy Trails and

Smiles for memories.

2018

WAR BETWEEN HEAVEN AND HELL IS OVER

Truly, it had everything to do with secrets,
Hell took over, but one left knowing all.
He traveled throughout to create all prophets,
Knowing very well that they'd drop the ball.

Those of control forgot they were being lead,
To confessing their ways to why they fled.
Beast brags on how strong the power becomes,
Cowering when feeling fumbled pleading weak.

Creations from nothing eventually becomes,
Bragged power, even though seeming week.
Sacrificed in hopes that they would remember,
Returning to claim as the first member.

A COUPLE'S FLIGHT

Missed, the moments of memories,
Found together centralized at will.
Totaled for heavy held stories,
At glances of the old iron mill.

Monuments of story placed on high,
And unmatched hair grows in tight.
Pillow patterns earns a single sigh,
While waves of deceit are in flight.

Seconds slip away to hours paired,
During laughter of new sights aware.
Lingered lays light curves carved,
But waking centers spread new air.

Become the soar that pleads the sky,
Catch couples in action with an eye.

DEATH'S HOME

If masked by plague's fortune,
   And denied the route of death.

Then hold you weather's tune,
   While maintaining your last breath.

Swallow the father's known religion,
   Pleading you knew him as Seth.

Fake future's lend towards Rome,
   Then unburied life will be home.

HOW INTERESTING

How interesting is the time of the earth?
Playing breaths piece to time a birth?
Clock-in to wage a year's worth,
As wandering feet slither around earth.

Weighted wanes catch eager eyes,
While whispers seek silent streams.
Pillow plagued for a juror's rise,
Punches blood throughout the streams.

A Rester's rest counts a beat,
As visions encompassed endured paths.
Annual earnings raises restless feet,
Blocking viral secrets surrounding baths.

How interesting depends on your rotation,
How interesting is the supplication?!

OPENED MOLD

Drifted markers pose for death's lie,
Keeping memory allowed to future's hold.
Why is it hard to say the last goodbye?
When can warmth finally unthaw the cold?

Thinned out tasks to a summer's melt,
Brings surfaced air aloof in a wane.
Together reunited to strap on the belt,
Wasting tears of the forsaken and insane.

Spring into forgotten days of wealth,
Carrying controlled climates of indoors.
Mask mountains of molded health,
And shifted sands of sunny shores.

Place the future towards yesterday's cry,
To open paths set out as we all fry.

THE NEXT STEP

As the sun shines brightly on my back,
I see a long, dark shadow on the ground.
Wondering if I will ever be on the right track,
I suddenly notice I'm the only on around.

I look towards the east and see a storm coming in,
Thinking now if this is the end.
I close my eyes and see nothing within,
Hoping that God will have something to send.

There's a cry of a wolf that opens my mind,
It blocks out the clouds and the sun shines right in.
My heartbeat sops and my eyes go blind,
Realizing now it's just time to begin.

THE FALLING LEAF

When was it last that my heart hurt so?
Where was the relentless effort of aid?
Many long unadventurous months go
By, and still the soil can not be laid.

While autumn winds increase in brute force,
Leeching leaves maintain their position.
Tied up with a haunted detoured course,
As re-routed dependents take altered action.

Yet, assistance is only an arm length away,
And earth is easily frolicked when joy permits.
Being cocooned has everlasting thoughts to say,
When inevitable change depicts where she sits.

The mind is altered by an historical pattern.
If past precedes present, then future does return.

LIVING BOLD

For in the ways when Cupid is Eros,
Together as one, each shore direction.
Passing all current to remain close,
Finding overlapped passes in reflection.
Mining minutes mimicking a mouse,
Molds minus in time of construction.

As centuries form to days untold,
Be confident, forever living bold.

INSIDE THE DEVIL'S HEAD

Inside the Devil's head we placed a piece,
Waiting for him to become fully complete.
Wanting a Wayne, he sat within a niece,
Believing we who need will not ever defeat.

Marked are they, if you have ever heard,
To old stories beaten as they are released.
Blessed are all who loved a nervous nerd,
For his time he stole and took out a lease.

Plagues of plunder devour the waking thunder,
For Sadie's sadness created all new wakes.
Whistles worry the crowd, placing them under,
A false charge which begins all new aches.

Faith from above helped a lonely sentence,
Developing heaven for those of true repentance.

BROTHER'S ONES AND ZEROS

Hiding away, dismissed in fear,
Within a being belonged to another.
Far traveled to produce a cheer,
Asking for assistance to stop brother.
Fives of port-holes brings us near,
To evil's plot to sacrifice the other.

Mismatched, deception switches ones,
Towards zero zipping silent runs.

THE RIGHT

Embark on a fainted fear forgotten,
Timber the willows of false statements.
Play pigs pen wanting it rotten,
Plagues ordained towards installments.

Mask mild mornings cultivating a mist,
Deregulating negative bold to there own.
Placing the power such that it is their fist,
Deems them regular to an original frown.

Concern asks any about truth to become,
And answers reveal without such a bomb.
Cower behind known towers at welcome,
Pleased and relieved, their will be no bomb.

Be it held for repentance holds the right,
Right of the right will always be the right.

DEUSE

The still roads of the listening night,
Leaves a path for the glistening light.
Although seeming bare and wide,
This road has a hell of a ride.

Fast trucking characters to whom thrill provide,
And to those whose might will be denied.
But there the force can show its light,
With acceleration, begins the fight.

Fast paced, one of many will take the lead,
Maintaining velocity and no room to bleed.
The thrill of defeat will cure the passage,
But have no reason to leave a message.

Let it roll through all the challenges it may,
Just remember in the end we all have to pay.

DEPRIVED

Depriving thoughts of the unknown,
Gives capital to our thrown.
While sweet. Oh! So sweet...
Questions gather at our feet.

Haste fulness, comes not from the sole,
But from the ministering hole.
Where righteousness takes our eye
And the truth is not a lie.

Yet, we deny all we are
And crucify all who we are.
Let grow what will; Leave all,
Who want, room for their ball.

A youthful thought could last a lifetime.
Depriving thoughts will destroy that time.
Laissez-faire! It's a good time.

HORIZONTAL FOOT

When are we out... of fields beyond?
Can we reach our plains by foot?

Travel North bending barriers of bond,
Balancing bubbles buried within the soot.

Flying after a good run bellowing "Yawned!"
Answers a longed remark of "You Idiot!"

Supplemental care coplanar the air,
For April's taste thaws horizontal air.

LIFE'S PIECE

To what degree will we be satisfied with peace?
No fighting? No arguing? Big brother's watch?
Spread out with many holding a piece,
Waiting and hoping to find the match.

Remembering days of old views at will,
Holding on to items we've already lost.
Baking goods are produced from the mill,
As mighty men take without any cost.

Letting go releases Love's path for return,
Counting the free has ancient abilities.
Noting what is yours, sets them to burn,
While moments emit and light qualities.

When a couple grasp time unseen,
They see the life that they have been.

LONG LOST BROTHER

We see through the looking glass,
A monumental picture presents.
Lawful glances on the mass,
Towards memories within tents.

Give mild tokens when you last saw,
A glare of essence that beautifies.
The moments lost during your thaw,
And that which was gathered by flies.

Playfully pang the pitted night,
As Revelation shows no borders.
Kiss the wounded for they did fight,
To memories when you gave orders.

Make yourself for they need laughter,
Allow them to remember the lost brother.

EDGE

Throughout time strengths have created a new,
And the claim has renewed that of is.
Questions squander about who has the shoe,
While knowledge crumbles to a smeared fizz.

Passing Power towards one who seemingly needs,
Believing that special is more than a word.
Delivering gifts of nature through many breeds,
And slowly modifying the mystification of a bird.

Passing moments of memory allows History to form,
But answering the call takes more than strength.
Deliverance comes together while feeling all warm,
Creating time and flyte to have great length.

A sole that fits holds more than knowledge,
Marking gifts places knowledge on the edge.

INVOLVING HAMMERS

Here, repeating a memory's thought,
Written down for an enjoyed plot.
Laughter recalled remembering all,
Who held on to see the fall.

Making time creating cracks-a-lot,
Revealing involved One's getting shot.
Passed allowance waiting on a call,
To join the masses for many a ball.

Spring's softness forms to summer's,
Way of protecting little left hammers.
Casting future in line for wealth,
Holds moments high hiring health.

Be back ready tokenned to receive,
Forgiven passes prolonged and believed.

FORTUNE'S HEALTH

Far from home waiting for fortune's tune,
Whistling away from wave's length.
A coated season will create a prune,
With laughter as its main strength.
Delivered be characters whom are in cartoon,
While listening to a lover's length.

Filter anticipated ways of wealth,
To maintain prosperity and health.

TONS OF ONES

Pictures left at doorsteps long forgotten,
And lamp's light still shines on no One.
Paste patterns proclaiming pale pangs,
While lust illuminates luggage lost.
Spring waste into captured moments,
But, forget returning plastic molds.

Ways of the memory counts on ones,
But, binary seconds add second tons.

TIMOTHY WAYNE RYDER

FARMER'S DIRECTION

Faith, placed in opposite directions,
Gives holes honored under certain steps.
Farmer's add to next year's conclusions,
And cloud formations perform in reps.

When we lie, our position is revealed,
Thanks to reason, we know about then.
As we dream, our mind becomes unpeeled,
And gifts of plenty surround a hen.

Aid for assistance still needs a rest,
For creations are only as good as they show.
Even in moments when at their best,
They can still be leveled with a blow.

Keep the truth known to be right,
While those above maintain our light.

MOUNTAIN FLOWER

Placed earnestly awaiting the paid thyme,
Filtered by blessings over Summer's summit.
Catch wind and lick luck to lime,
Passing October blind revealing an omit.
Allow pressing people luxury of rhyme,
When crooked cocks cure curds wit.

Pissing in wind counts as no clean shower,
But cold run-offs will levi to flower power.

MASK

Differentiated, see ourselves in another sole,
Desperate to believe we live the life of others.
Holding on to origins of those in the hole,
·Waking to a midnight full of other brothers.

Can we develop into One's who truly believe?
When can we breath through our own lung?
A mask that has been passed without eve,
Has uncured moments of lust and long.

Forgiving our trespassers allows later hope,
While sibling matters breath hatefully.
Slowly dawning on the undiscovered dope,
Trusts a quick apple to be revealed fully.

Be willing to give into your alternate self,
Be you, not he and you will always be yourself.

MOVING BEER

Breathtaking, we climb stairs for wear.
The energy released brightens the light.
Will the move be finished without a beer?
Can they work together without a fight?

Climbing from case to case fades an eye,
While picture of blunder ride the rail
Keeping the motion during a long tie,
Fakes a delivery of a cold hard ale.

Movements of must are warmed in handing,
For shots are taken to unsure the payment.
Hold on tight until you reach the landing,
While acceptance fills the air with scent.

When assisting in trouble in time or near,
Accept the movements without any beer.

SUNDIAL SONG

Walking in the way of the sundial,
Our feet harden to days unseen.
Pushing numbers towards a file
Brings blame to those foreseen.

Making distance with a laughter,
Holds many by the roadside.
Cupping songs together, we are after,
And meat for all on the side.

Dishes were found as useful tools,
While moods tell time aloud.
Closer are we who place the rules,
For cleaning currency has us proud.

Marked for days of joy and wonder,
Singing songs we cure our ponder.

CELESTIAL DREAM

Marveled with time with an untracked mind.
Distanced by religion and those we can not find.
Where in the unnatured do we find love?
Is it where dreams come from? Up above?

Knowledge without action screams with delight.
Passion without courage curses people at night.
If you look you can see the expression as they pass.
Don't look too hard cause it'll kick you in the ass.

Fear is a privilege that people endure.
When it's at your doorstep, you pray for a cure.
There is celestial reasoning that brings out hope.
There is no need for a ladder if enough hold the rope.

It's in our dreams that life seems so real.
It's in our lives that dreams seem so real.

D.A.R.R.Y.L.

Desperate, we grudge sloppy seconds,
Filtered by waves of ill minded Ones.
Where do we search to find the end?
Can we return them for refunds?

Miss matched alike turning for wear,
Those buttons pressed leave prints.
Turning to others, who have no care,
Believing all crumbs left as hints.

Dimensional characters live in dust,
Arrays capture their form allowed.
Revisited moments determine a must,
Remembering all the struggles towed.

Your truth carries you through it all,
Lies make you have to crawl.

THE POTATOE

Where in a word can enough be said?
Is justice redeemed with apologized speech?
Mother nature plows the flower bed,
And trees bloom an apple, cherry and a peach.

Heat fills June with a melancholic beet,
And the rented summer betrays belief.
As molten thoughts are released through streets,
Heavy dirt compiles beyond relief.

Yet, dignified moments present an ease,
And laboured diligence creates a reward.
Kinder action reduces need for please,
While chilled avenues generate an orchard.

Toward tomorrow many spud will grow,
Throughout eternity many more will show.

WIFE OF A LIFE

Nesting to a wanted way of fun,
Dreaming of mellow birds at dusk.
Melting tingles cooking a bun,
Pasting friends, who had a tusk.
Washing years you had to run,
Flees the scent most call musk.

Wrestle a deer to join in life,
Missing true life without a wife.

UNGUIDED

Too many times misfortune by twisting environment.
Baffled into change of unguided rearrangement.
Directed by media ideals which contradict tradition.
Now plagued with offspring who require meditation.

Masked by virtuous lust in a time of a cronic rush.
The aged see their flaws while education hides a bush.

To liveth with boundaries that
Has been left before you.
Is to cherish the moment and
The family that calls and adore you.

Take heart and time uncompleted
And allow its message to be undeleted.

TIME IN HELL

Spotted to move in a fixed direction,
Now forced to fulfill a structured pill.
Be it wound with sufficient collection,
And basted along side the iron will.
Paste the picture in rear view reflection,
To penetrate all the days as a spill.

Filtered by force, the light became well.
Time keeps going, even if you call it hell.

LOST AT THIRTY TWO

Currently of the age thirty-two, I fornicate,
Squandering my Bi-polar with schizo-effectiveness.
Living away from home searching for an eight,
Blissful knowing I have completed love's loneliness.
Remembering University's lessons, wanes a wait,
While working weigh's weight on our happiness.

Cupping a tarnished glass blessed to be full,
Holds moments of wonder within the skull.

YOU LOSE

In the mounted ways of a starry clear,
The voices echo without a fluted cheer.
They keep wandering away from themselves,
Too ashamed to commit themselves.

Basting in another's toiled will,
Bragging about someone who took a pill.
Bitter sweet! They now lie at your feet,
For charmed they were; they did not defeat.

Swim to them and reveal a message,
Today unlocked an age old passage.
Playing games in all types of weather,
Making sure they wear some leather.

Pick or choose because you always lose.
Remember the fight you could not lose.

OVER THE DON'T

Dream the dreams of yesterday's calling,
And reveal the flyte that paved your way.
Answer any questions while you are falling,
In order to paste the future in your way.

Give to anyone who seems your taste,
And forgive the fortune that trails.
We all laugh, live and love in waste,
While we argue over all broken tales.

Far be it for me to anoint someone special,
But musts are musts and lead to failing.
Could we now be at one with one another,
Helping and caring over all the other?

In that time or anytime, we shall lend a hand,
And know if we do, we do; if we don't, we don't.

TIMOTHY WAYNE RYDER

ONE STEP TO THE NEXT

One step
Embarking on a privilege,
Allowing us to fulfill our promise.
Honours our heart,
Plagues the desire.
Fulfills the glory of watchfulness,
Completing an old story
To next step.

CLAIMING THE BLAME

Sitting down spilling hearts on paper,
Wasting indoors craving new lessons.
Beating the way to an age old caper,
Rooting the dawn of unmatched seasons.

Casting favours to unforgiven sides,
Holding ink back for later proof.
Making rhythms restless for rides,
Rigging rails for a tumbling roof.

While making and faking your ways,
Maintain your wear, you cannot bear.
During the waking hours of the maze,
Follow the feeling, if you cannot hear.

When the written words make claim,
Open your arms to take the blame.

AWKWARD CURE

Awkward, leaving love behind,
Praying the power has learned.
Fear not for memories remind,
Individual steps once were burned.

Kissing an old fool on the behind,
Realizing forgiven duties earned.
Many laugh when change occurs,
Many dread the age old cures.

BEAUTIFUL EARTH

We're from earth,
We are multicultural.
We're from earth,
We're all from the universe.
We're from earth,
We are all so beautiful.
We're from earth,
We are multicultural.
We're from earth,
Our King's and Queen's are beautiful.
How we have all become,
So beautiful.

GREAT BLUE

When in a time of ice and snow,
Be sure to cover between spaces.
Know it now, it is going to blow,
For some have feet in the races.

Blessed be tows towards the red nose,
And walks which occur during the night.
'Cause limbs have fallen into a pose,
While eyes watch the endurable fight.

Pick and choose while you can do,
And hold your place that calls to you.
Mild suns wait for the right shoe,
During the view from the great blue.

Maintain the course which you set out,
Then next time you won't sit out.

FORGOTTEN PICTURES

When you see finely with your heart,
Then your eyes see ugly as beautiful.
Conquer pasted memories melting art,
Wasting away all ailments as blissful.
Winning divine devices deemed smart,
Marked a mask presented as "wiskful."

Re-gain the realm remained rotten,
To possess painted pictures forgotten.

FOR MY DEAR HUN

What is a fair word for my dear hun?
Could a gentle breeze describer her touch?
The month of June is almost done,
And without a word I've done too much.

A falling leaf will hit the ground,
With the silence of soft to fall upon.
To lose or to find; to be lost or found,
The fragrance will reach across the lawn.

Within two months I've gained my feel,
Waiting upon the arrow to reach the heart.
When paths do cross, I to you shall kneel,
Which will join us until death do us part.

If my lines are hummed to rhyme
The life of love has no time.

SINCERE THANKS

In days of past discussion,
My ways got the best of me.
Filtering an old conclusion,
Realizing, we all help me.
For when we are inappropriate,
It is easy to exclude others.
Remembering how much we ate,
Cures a passage for our mothers.
Blessed are they of patience,
Knowing a plan is still there.
Place your truth at Hense,
Accepting, we will be there.
Forgive me for past recognition,
Today we understand repetition.

FIGHT FOR JOY

When in the arms of carefree days,
Take heart and hope along to view.
Many memories that make-up a maze,
For helping some takes only a few.

Be it here or there; be it now or later,
Smiles of laughter create friends abroad.
A wink of an eye, trails a sour tear,
While voices about, cast out the rod.

The "catch of the day" tastes bitter sweet,
'Cause solutions of plenty cloud the day.
An enemy's offering lays at your feet,
And crying of joy, presents them gay.

When the glimmer of light shines bright,
Know that there, we have won the fight.

THE WAY OF THE GROUT

In the closet of coldness,
There was beauty of oldness.
Many mates and lots of
Company to endure a wait.
The time came near
And united without a fear.
There stood time's way
To produce altered play.

SPENDING PATH

Wondrous, a path made for a hike,
Sets on a course meant to be free.
Bumping blunders blind bats alike,
As the leaves fall from the tree.

A coupled log holds feet in the way,
While invited insects host a bite.
Cocooned critters should bloom in May,
But counting cooks grasp the fight.

Spread out hands for glorious days,
The road often bumps in expectant.
A month away to pair bugs away,
For break outs occur at an entrant.

If you rise to view the ending,
You will cry and reduce spending.

THE TREES THAT FORMED CUPID'S ARROWS

Cold, we stand and wait our turn,
Swaying and swearing in the wind.
What time do we reveal our shape?
When can the children finally unwind?

Two crosses have been left in ashes,
And the search is only but half way.
Classes form to determine the bows,
While adults cast riches in their way.

Seconds and hours pass by unannounced,
And research helps to strike the match.
Ringing bells determine wind direction,
While the youth bundle up in warmth.

Shooting stars have a moment to be.
Stationary though, will be left to be.

WRONG SONG

Redirected in boundless glory,
Gratifying mentors of reason.
Fills our minds; tells a story.
Be ready for the changed season,
As history remembers gory.
Forward moving helps an age on,
A forgotten myth of years gone wrong.

Together now, we create a song.
Be it later, we can't go wrong.

PRESENT VINE

Jaded pictures of a New Year's pledge,
Leaves passion at hand for tomorrow.
Lessons fulfilled at a step and edge,
Placing nature at lend for borrow.

Masking attempts to present nude,
Brings mellow feathers to be plucked.
Upon request the anointed are rude,
And the arrested blood is sucked.

Offered ways fear the present strip,
While anger pays the growing vine.
Plus or minus; birds make the trip,
Altering frames of the printed line.

When at the mind of days less had,
Press learn and gather to be glad.

A MINER MAID'S SON

Made a mind molded for maids,
Placing pale pinned pictures for pay.
Quest's query captures quite raids,
For affordable fights figure a way.

Want haunts the pillows to sway,
Capping pens at the printed notion.
Filtering men mentioning their play,
Opens the idea of the aged potion.

Milk spills and forms as a puddle,
Crammed ailments defend arrangement.
To be mopped; mopped as subtle,
As re-arranged, it becomes a cuddlement.

Mild minutes form to become told,
Age old miners mimicking a son sold.

LAUGHTER BETWEEN MARS AND VENUS

Midnight chatter looms lunar light,
Mixing moments waxed for a wane.
Coupled laughter lingering might,
To release old prolonged pain.
Sipping softly towards true right,
Receives gifts forgotten as gain.
Given ways helped paved the ways,
Towards remembering colden sways.

CLEAN BUCKET

Fortified by particulars to receive
Questions abilities of tomorrow
And whether you were a Queen.

Barriers cause the lot to deceive
A poisoned bucket for borrow.
As destitute go forward unseen.

Steady rest to become clean.

PLAYYING CARDS

Placing all the Devils in one Heep,
Running for the entrance hoping to exit.
A load of friends come from sheep,
Now sides are even as elders sit.

Satan's gun fires multicolours of red,
Turning eyes to power that light limbs.
Realizing everyone around is now dead,
They cock open to reveal shinny rims.

Playying with plenty of injury free,
Denotes coloured cards for your hierarchy.
When shuffled red turns to black,
To remember someone has your back.

Partner's paired towards experience redone,
Your enemy is a friend and all are one.

SHADOW MESSAGE

Faint, the shadow of the moon is lite,
For innocence dropped the rubber ball.
Flavour hearted to maintain might,
As River's read inside a local mall.

Can youth dance and play in unity?
Will they always run home to mom?
Elder siblings and friends show pity,
Because big brother created a bomb.

Being in wise shelters holds a roof,
And tasteful music ranges across lands.
Someone will always find proper proof,
For dry valley walks blow in sands.

What a way to fill an unheated message,
Denote figures to clear a passage.

UNSIMILAR

Placed unmatched for wear,
Sipping on beer by a fire.
To early sometimes we hear,
The beautiful sounds of the choir.
Chilled evening produce a gear,
For old hands try to hire.

Unalike we share our truths,
Helping each other maintain true.

TIMOTHY WAYNE RYDER

WHISTLE PLAY

Two wings pour the silent soup,
Shaping molds melting cured dye.
Whistles sound developing a group,
Together matching mysteries made cry.

Fortified fountains forgiving fallacy,
Heating figures counting the flight.
Miniature wakes mend a sea,
For passer by motion gained sight.

Fists held sturdy, saving Saturday,
Revealing completion, so let us play.

YESTERDAY'S LOSS

What maintenance will the hair gray?
When will wrinkles spread out thin?
Harlem winds cast tomorrow to be prey,
While others search for the found pin.

Mounting surplus sparks many dough,
When honourary hells cast them on fire.
Leaving many loose; they still do owe,
A silent patient, listening to the choir.

Forces delivered to a beast's brag unknown,
Reeling in shelter, where bumps are pebbles.
Citing mountains of wisdom, we now own,
And educated searches, that's left as fables.

Cling on tight to yesterday's loss,
Be held tomorrow ready for a toss.

MOLTEN RIVER OF HEAVEN

When the soothing Sultan begins,
Air is filled of uttering loneliness.
Music melts the fruits of the tree,
To wither away until with Lockness.

Beaten quarries relent a sweet glare,
For those who carry monumental stairs.
Determined to release ailments to air,
In steps produce Autumn's new pairs.

Contingency allows a breath from earth,
Feeding birds aware who perch high in air.
Mountains hold dear a child for birth,
As melodies harden a new foundation heir.

Molten rivers climb far and near,
Towards a feeling that heaven is here.

MISS ART

Sincere, forgetful thoughts held tight,
Leaving behind the joy of old lands.
Helpful hands prove to be right,
While laughing lords stop the bands.

A self-righteous sigh presents wonder,
As children kinder to collection dues.
Students gather to enjoy a ponder,
When a missed teacher cries the blues.

Corrected amounts pave youth to go,
Towards professions of released desire.
Collected nic-nac's brings grins to show,
For a hand was paid to raise a choir.

Cry and sing through days of heart,
Come together, be revealed as art.

MISSING TIME

What kind of brute can one man become?
To what knowledge will he leave behind?
Being left in the cold to raise a thumb,
Or setting a clock with the proper wind.

Raising the cattle on old whipped hay,
And bruising a brother at the lieu.
Mysteries promote mothers to sway,
While lessons learned are but a few.

We have but our turn to point a finger,
During solutions solved of missing crops.
Matured wisdom sets thrones to linger,
While elders heal warmth with mops.

Bring forth a winding clock by day,
To notion a time which will stay.

OLD BEING TOLD

Gathering collection of rain
Prepared to fall.
Clogged the path became
Bankrupting a mall.
Long held were the riches
To celebrate a ball.

Sighted memories of dwellings
Earn new born gold.
Caught up in elders claim
The children become bold.
Now youth plays the part
Where the old become told.

PATIENT AGE

Why do we leave patience to start forever?
Could we live with less on our plates?
Many miles are laid by notions of never,
During games of whether you held eights.

Passing figures through holes allowed,
Paying purposes to forgive the pass.
Leaking layers lend labour to owed,
Pleading opposites to refill the gas.

Eternity's shift starts before they begin,
While ordered hands stop the dripping.
Placing of power positions a pale grin,
During lessons laughed of them pretending.

Lick your thumb and count your pages,
For there is a way of knowing the ages.

ME TO YOU

Within all the days of passing time,
Love has but, only one solution.
Lustful chores create lots of rhyme,
While sensuous cuddling creates emotion.

Hastefullness, poured from a bottle,
And the glass barely goes empty.
Midnight chatter stirs up a rattle,
Morning breaks, the query was plenty.

Me to you, I have no other,
Our time together breaks any record.
To wound a feeling, I'd rather not bother,
Yet resent actions occur, but I am no Lord.

We survive together, we understand.
Our lives together are in great demand.

LONG AND THE SHORT

Does hair grow long to determine sex?
Will the apple be plucked from the tree?
Crushing cans make a sniveler flex,
While a river floods up to the knee.

White, black, gray, and all the same, we
Scratch our itch to stop our healing.
Nuclear fission fades all towards thee,
But catching our fish gives feeling.

Making metal pours proper pangs,
As atoms released rights wrists aware.
Questioning colours regain the gangs,
When similar wounds start to beware.

All on a watch for fuzzy fruits,
Can shortly wait to become brutes.

KIN GRIN

On a mist of open glory,
Paving pathways to success.
Callous the used story,
For aged create fusses.

Deemed credit hollows a debt,
When watchful ears pay touch.
Linking others obtains a pet,
Assisting ails from future's crutch.

Weather determined for day's rest,
Allowing walks of continuous talk.
Mixed emotions put up a test,
Mellowing youth playing with chalk.

Give well to develop your kin,
Marking memories forming a grin.

NIGHT LIGHT

Shining stars know of effort,
To believe in our right to shine.
New efforts erect a cool fort,
While many say "It is mine."
Settled are discussions in a court,
To render missions as fine.

Kicked back and relaxed at night,
We recognize our new found light.

EXTENTION

Drifting away in a time of motionless desires,
Basting in lawfulness when gray turns to white.
To far to hear the soothing sounds of the choirs,
To close to feel the pounding pain of spite.

How far is the distance where heaven is safe?
Will the fuel of power levi to a side less taken?
Much trouble has been prevented within a safe,
Many fear the distant road not yet taken.

Music of many finds its way to the perimeters,
And wisdom will discover how to unlock paths.
New roads have been formed by meteors,
While old energy solves the mysterious myths.

Feel comfort when your moment brings harm,
Know that someone will always extend their arm.

WEATHERED FLESH

Hollowed, they dissect me from inside,
Watching overboard to drift with ease.
Caught in a current flowing with a tide,
Damaged waters cause a beach to ease.

Everything in, is now out in the wide open,
Placing nothing nowhere and something everywhere.
Are great moments lost until they happen?
Could they possibly be at a worse for wear?

Mindful memories caused from dreadful deeds,
Mimic historical patterns past by hands.
Whether or not we have pulled all the weeds,
Best waters always dry up in the sands.

Until salt from the sea turns all to fresh,
Maintain your ways and all of your flesh.

THE IMPOSSIBLE MILE   (A.E.I.O.U.)

(Back to the Basics...)

Distance finds its way between us,
Yielding perimeters not seen in years.

Travel in the weighed turns, "Ofabus,"
For the towel comes to dry the tears.

Depend on true strength of the truss,
While area maintains our gears.

When counting on the forgotten mile,
That's when "It" will still take a while.

BY THE LIGHT

Blessed, he of righteousness,
Pondered by gatherings and treasure.
Casts the day in lawlessness,
By searching for a cure.
Haunted by the light,
He will always have sight.

DAY

To be on a day full of perpetuating lust,
Holding on to granulars of sharp edges.
Using this day, it is troubling to find crust,
And mounting trust which we give pledges.

Hold off momentarily while forces remain,
On punishment of the lost and long forgotten.
Must this day grow older with such pain?
Will time come when it is not all rotten?

Set your hand down where it is most fitting,
Fate has honourable hindsight out on a limb.
Hold it close to you for it may be running,
While strengths balance itself holding the brim.

Bless the day, we have liberty and are free,
Grasp light to remember this will always be.

TIMOTHY WAYNE RYDER

PECHED DOVE

To see;
The dove perched quietly in the air,
Holding on to reconciliation of a tear.
Friendly horns pass without a stare,
Being led to somewhere just to hear.
Touched by those of the deserved,
Keeping form allowed and reserved.
To live.

SHINING MIGHT

Fixing repairs broken for wear,
Leads us to foundations at dusk.
Placing pillow patterned fear,
Admits lost, left behind a tusk.
Washing away a long lost tear,
Helps forgive an age old husk.

Fixed moonlight shines bright,
As molten memories maintain might.

SNOW TALE

How much thanks can one extend to another?
Is it easier to offer a hug or a simple flower?
There's so much a person can to when their better
And time only allows for good or bad weather.

Too many times snow comes to present a coat,
With a soft white pillow that tempts your senses.
Often you are urged to follow the river boat,
Which leads to freedom and is blocked by fences.

For all that I have and all that you offer,
A good night sleep can make one feel better.
Temperature changes and climate too,
When I am close to you I rarely feel blue.

Time has its way of curing an ail,
If that doesn't work, just tell a tale.

SEASON'S MILE

Might I hold the grounded wood?
May many free flowers find their way?
The grass of June has turned to mud,
And autumn's fruit times the play.

Broken arrows bleed through pain,
While an armoured message gets caught.
Water to snow; then snow to rain,
Through it all, we have fought.

When peaceful grains hold the might,
And mended wounds laughed together.
There a speech glamours the right,
For season's plague we all weather.

Break into the month with smiles,
Accepting, we all walked many miles.

TIMOTHY WAYNE RYDER

FORGIVEN FETCH

Feet forgiven of understood paths,
Forsakes reason to attend a ball.
Cleanliness comes during the baths,
As wealth shares at a local mall.
Bring joy completing myth-ed maths,
Joining together to reduce a fall.

Miss matched to enjoy a fetch,
Gives reason for a child's etch.

COMPLETE

The mist of the white, puffy clouds had been replenished
The mist commenced to relieve the sour drops of water.
The water started dashing downwards.
The water pitter-pattered on the rooftops.
The drops began gathering on the surface.
The drops had taken the form of a puddle.
The puddle had a unique wake upon its surface.
The puddle had seized to produce waves.
The water had begun to evapourate.
The water became as one with the surface.
The mist that once formed a white, puffy cloud.
The mist that has vanished from the earth.

CAUSE COURSE

Tempered, drifting place loses sight,
As symbols drain out hidden ways.
Pacific glory gains wisdom and might,
As starboard views catches all the waves.

Mystified moonlight shows no remorse,
Placing people below for sanity and shelter.
Moving moments to maintain the cause course,
Fighting filters and filming the Helter skelter.

An astonishing eye calms many meters,
While clouds clutter the lunar light.
Saving souls remembers insane waters,
For carried sterns forget a fogged fight.

Planks walked toward an endless glory,
Lifts lingered moments to an endless story.

PLAY, PLAY

Hypnotic laughter sets art for days,
When a lying Lucifer embarks a toil.
Could enough strength prevent sways?
Will their car be filled with oil?

Questions answered during pill intake,
And children smile for brother's way.
Luster love may endure the break,
Because psycho play now must pay.

Easy calm fills times lamp with fire,
While young emotion flex the passage.
Smiling horns bill later that tire,
For play is play that needs a message.

Carry those to when they pleaded,
Notion us for when we defeated.

FAMILY REIGN

When was it last that the snow fell?
Do the Gods punish us without?
Looking around wondering about hell,
We cast ourselves holding in a shout.

Dry heat plagues the noon day sun,
As melted memories drain our mind.
Be it clear, we're living away from fun,
And tomorrow develops us all blind.

Guided colds relieve sights abroad,
While clouded life whispers in joy.
Father stands to produce the nod,
For the sitting son's reign does annoy.

Plead through lands of disliked values,
Join together to produce family values.

SIMMER SILENT HILL

Destitution excepted as forgiveness,
While beauty falls in future's will.
Accepting smile's simmer silent duress,
For neighbouring knees collect a spill.
Fortune recovered to create a mindless mess,
Propelling anger against an adjacent hill.

Minding memories long rested in dust
Peaks our duty to fulfill a must.

CROWN'S FULFILLMENT

Snowed in footprints remind a renege,
Cautioning whispered plans at dusk.
Momentary members throw many a egg,
Washing winter swallowing a heavy husk.

Flipped, twisted and turned upside down,
Regrets filter why decisions are made.
Power hungry to wear an achieved crown,
Pasted all loved to function as a maid.

Long hours and deep thinking seconds,
Create voiced direction dreaming summer.
Indigent fellow writes of forgotten funds,
Bonding patterns as many morning simmer.

Pleased are creations to dwell in moment,
Directing evil to remember their fulfillment.

DISFUNCTIONED

Lost, within a domain of reasoning time,
Discovering no will for all possible rhyme.
Knowing all of little by just playing a fiddle,
And that of what has been left in the middle.

For all of you, all of I, of it and all of them,
Formation among is indescribable without a gem.
Felling behind is uncaused and unjust,
For being a being, it is simply just a must.

Be what you will; be what you may,
But in the end you may or may not have to pay.
Then, of course, there is reason of total sound and body.
Is it right for you? Will it cure the melody?

Peace of what is, may not all be what possibly could be.
While knowing what is, has limitation on what will be.

EACH AND EVERY DAY

Quistful, in my ways of launder,
Basting in oil of unboiled fuel.
Questioning that of the ponder,
Mentions metal molded masking a mule.
If my time has cured a wonder,
Moments cuddle those of a fool.

Meek the wood whittled of wonder,
Passing them who still wander.

MOMENT TO MOMENT

Tired, the moments of memories lost,
Found broken without prolonged will.
Puzzled for a mystical morning frost,
When guild gagged and forced a pill.
Present mornings defy deaf debts,
Plus, mighty midnights mawke a will.

Squander moments allowed to be yours
For when they are mine...

MIRACLE CIRCLE

Baffled by brilliant charms of colden years,
Millennium markers leave wood at dusk.
Mystical moments flee intolerable fears,
To add trophies abroad without a tusk.

Do our sacrifices complete yesterday's call?
Should books designate the underline?
When the hand bleeds ready to fall,
And brother's unite to cross the line.

The traveled trail leaves a thousand sites,
Where life breeds willing to warm a tooth.
Pages flipped about soaring like kites,
Leaving today held high at dawn's booth.

Unannounced the lines scare the circle,
Pronounced the circle becomes a miracle.

PATIENT BREATH

In deft ears does my mind remind,
Of old cloth hung out to lather.
When conscious, ladder becomes blind,
For tenderness put up a bother.
Cowered away, protecting the kind,
Waiting restless for the pass of brother.

Smitten to fall at Autumn's breath,
Patiently stepping away for breath.

FEARING THE WAY

Hardened habits haunt the watched hour,
Playing fool to the mind, draining the old.
Cupping jesters to drink away the sour,
And laughing lawless to mortaring mold.
Fainted eyes open, diminishing a devour
While wise wishes wash a story told.

Following delight cast by fear's way,
Swallows a hole revealing a new way.

FUN HAPPENS

During walks of ponder,
Historical patterns remind.
Times which we wonder,
On our duty to give a wind.

Set forth towards a plain,
Honouring maintained tasks.
Protected inside from rain,
To uncover the masks.

Ask to join, the fun happens
As an accepted door opens.

AGAIN AND AGAIN

Which way does a heart lead?
Can the mind alter its course?
Inevitable occurrences will bleed,
Questioning many of no remorse.

Pasted freely to oversee the need,
Pumping valve outwards to receive.
Gathered within to fill the seed,
Motioned among to believe.

Catch on to the pour of the vein,
Releasing an order to fulfill order.
A view from within copying the reign,
Flows ponder, captivating the shorter.

Given to receive as to give again,
Memories maintain again and again.

ENDLESS LOVE

By way of belief
A charcoal buffer floats by,
Asking questions of non-relief.
Many query the notion fly
Feeling relieved to wave good-bye.
Thank the One from the reef,
Missing lines as a thief.
Mistakes help us cry
Thank you for the good bye.
Old sacrifice
Helped pave a way
Towards true glory.
Initiates pangs of love,
Embarks on endless love.

CROWN OF THE TREE

Countless ways of the plus or minus,
Awaits fevers pitched to days on end.
Lemons to lime to cure a clogged sinus,
Pays toll a plenty while pleading lend.

Coughing costs break father to tread,
Saving a virgins rest coated with feathers.
Can the fields form to enough bread?
Will the waters take away the brothers?

Messes mowed formulates a calm field,
During chopping of weighted cherry trees.
Missed kin mends metal making a shield,
For eyes to wake while willows freeze.

When you rise above the fallen down,
Hold your head high and wear the crown.

DEVELOPED FEATHER

Beautiful Earth where we became
So beautiful, distanced by sight,
The gatherings developed a name.
Flattering each others molded might.
Left at night children share blame,
For youth's memories create a fight.

Missed and matched puzzled together,
On a walk to discover a feather.

HEATED MIME

Stellar callings tempts eyes to flame,
When bright beads fill the sky.
Altered moons force pointed blame,
As people ponder and question why.

Aimless, we set our sights on high,
Awaiting forgiveness, we sit and cry.
Cold hand rest upon a higher thigh,
Please! Don't make us say good-bye.

Warmth, welcomes us all on our own,
While patterned pictures present light.
Two for one, we'll clean this town,
With heated hells and no fight.

When this rhyme finds the time,
Then you are mine to be a mime.

TRUTH

So much of the wait, do I sit
On the end on mine, when they'll come.
Terrible news from the west will admit,
Only enough to ensure where they're from.

Surprises and jackpots fill the the air,
While the free search for truth.
Will they live forever in dishonesty?
What will they do to find their truths?

There is a niche when freedom finds your mind,
It remembers origins and that what you are from.
Time is of essence while the clear does remind,
The heart knows but the mind depicts the from.

Lead your mind to where your heart shows.
Be it now, not then, then never won't show.

SANE CANDLE

Lighting ends of a pre-lit candle,
Wastes effort that lies between.
Why does only one hold the handle?
Where can we finally be seen?

A ball held high minioned to fall,
Leaves pieces a mist in fall places.
Gelled together the structure is tall,
While hands cover all our faces.

A short while longer towards a home,
During collection of old hand-outs.
Many see how everything has grown,
Uniting the wane to release the shouts.

"Come wither! Come wane! Live in vane!"
Say it all together to become insane.

WINTER'S FIRE

Melted winter's prepare the thaw,
Leaping memories to spring's raw.
Captured are they of the deceased,
Future's toll calms the great eased.
Playmate's couple the longed desire,
Grasping lures left in a flat tire.

Wish for a time to complete desire,
Continue along to maintain the fire.

FAITH

When do souls defeat definition of everyday?
Is it in the void, where they often pretend?
Boisterous, react on questions which they pray,
And yesterday's that define ways to an end.

Caught up in a world of lies and deceit,
Surrounded by those who have an eye for greed.
Forgetful are them, that scramble for a receipt,
And the One's whose colour is in desperate need.

What a life! When everyday is a Saturday!
Fills your holes while sustaining life around.
If the tint grows whole, red will be the day,
Then all credit clears to memories found.

Create a day of lust and keep the faith.
Belong together to maintain altered faith.

TIMOTHY WAYNE RYDER

TICKET

Feathered through shores of rocky shelves,
Distanced by peers and family the same.
Does Santa really have all those elves?
Should I point finger towards blame?

As a stubbed toe turns a face to red,
Infants run with smiles and laughter.
A story awaits bedside, hoping to be read,
As a barn lamb is scheduled for slaughter.

Answer in riddles to protect the truth,
Flip the frowns when you take aim.
Remark the ticket colour from the booth,
As a lie says that poles are in flame.

Closer are we who smooth the surfaces,
Forever allowed, a smile on our faces.

ILLUMINATING FATE

In midst of the moonlight,
There was a line of light.
Sparkling with wondrous joy,
Deemed for life as a toy.
Playful jolly dips do create,
Fun filled falls to enjoy a mate.
Challenges deem adventure to grow,
Uphill towards a miraculous show.

When glanced upon we illuminate,
To join together and seal our fate.

A VOLUNTEER'S STORY

When traveled from above as a flake,
Cold whispers cushion the awaited.
Mystified moments prevent a wake,
Blasted tunes push to be mated.

Twisted ailments caution the winter,
Allowing February's thaw towards conclusion.
Single arrows break into a splinter,
Causing paired lovers to match seclusion.

Wishful lusts unite forming a must,
Playing Joy's time splashing substance.
Dangerous falls produce a cured rust,
While slings of passion join a dance.

Ask to venture among the open glory,
Volunteer and receive an age old story.

LEVEL OF POWER

Making decisions based on pondering notions,
Lifts credit to levels of maximum plateaus.
Exceeding the bar without the aided potions,
While tip-toeing without stepping on any toes.

Alive, I bend myself for those who care,
Leaving only a mark in re-place of a need.
Relentless trouble comes from far and near,
During a motionless time when the uncared bleed.

Believe in a power that has ancient origins,
Curse to those against; bless the others.
Allow straightened time to level the grins,
And decide your scar colour of the feathers.

Place a finger on achievements of great,
Remove and move on to higher levels of fate.

A PenNY

One was enough to employ the world.
When was one enough?
A pen is one that helped you understand.
With one what would you have done?

FATHER, SON AND THE HOLY GHOST (THE FIGHT)

As the child of January crosses the chilling river,
Peace and harmony protect, but the whistles blow.
While an honest prediction is made that he may shiver,
Sudden whispers of light ease the procrastinating glow.

Pushing forward there is obvious doubt concerning mortality,
Creating lives and cracks without any hesitation.
Suggesting Messiah form while continuing with brutality,
Aiming closer, closer and closer to destruction.

As lightening bolt cracks furiously between his feet,
The vicious vulture screeks and the dove swiftly swims.
The child unwillingly skips every other beat,
As the "threshold of consciousness brims."

Flowing down with the currents of racing time,
He is often injured by rocks or colliding water.
In hope that someone has tasted a lime,
He reaches out with a beckoning cry for pater.

There's branches to the left and one to the right,
None of which are in his reach.
Continuing on, he slowly loses might,
While the strong river acts like a leach.

The forces are great and he is weak,
He sees darkness, but denies defeat.
If he hold his breath for just one week,
Then his flesh and bones will not be meat.

While his vision is darkened and his lungs are full,
His mind drifts into an ease.
There is a voice so warm, caring and beautiful,
Saying "the fight for life can never freeze."

Printed in Canada